A Guide for Using

Walk Two Moons

in the Classroom

Based on the novel written by Sharon Creech

This guide written by **Melissa Hart, M.F.A.**

Teacher Created Resources, Inc.
6421 Industry Way
Westminster, CA 92683
www.teachercreated.com
ISBN: 978-0-7439-3160-1
©2003 Teacher Created Resources, Inc.
Reprinted, 2008
Made in U.S.A.

Edited by
Walter Kelly, M.A.

Illustrated by
Howard Chaney

Cover Art by
Wendy Chang

Table of Contents

Introduction

A good book can enrich our lives like a good friend. Fictional characters can inspire us and teach us about the world in which we live. We can turn to books for companionship, entertainment, and guidance. A truly beloved book may touch our lives forever.

Great care has been taken with Literature Units to select books that are sure to become your students' good friends!

Teachers who use this unit will find the following features to supplement their own ideas:

- Sample Lesson Plans

- Pre-reading Activities

- A Biographical Sketch and Picture of the Author

- A Book Summary

- Vocabulary Lists and Suggested Vocabulary Activities

- Chapters grouped for study with each section including:

    —quizzes

    —hands-on projects

    —cooperative learning activities

    —cross-curricular connections

    —extensions into the reader's life

- Post-Reading Activities

- Book Report Ideas

- Research Activities

- Culminating Activities

- Three Different Options for Unit Tests

- Bibliography

- Answer Key

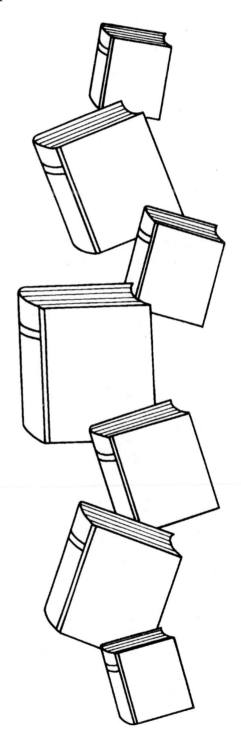

We are certain this unit will be a valuable addition to your own curriculum ideas to supplement *Walk Two Moons*.

Sample Lesson Plan

The time it takes to complete the suggested lessons below will vary, depending on the type of activity, your students' abilities, and their interest levels.

Lesson 1

- Introduce and complete some or all of the pre-reading activities from "Before the Book." (page 5)
- Read "About the Author" with students. (page 6)
- Introduce the vocabulary list for Section 1. (page 8)

Lesson 2

- Read Chapters 1–11. Discuss vocabulary words, using the book context to discern meanings.
- Locate Bybanks (Quincy), Kentucky, and Euclid, Ohio, on a map.
- Choose a vocabulary activity to complete. (page 9)
- Make blackberry pie. (page 11)
- Practice braille. (page 12)
- Make a map. Enlarge as needed. (page 13)
- Describe your mother. (page 14)
- Administer the Section 1 Quiz. (page 10)
- Introduce the vocabulary list for Section 2. (page 8)

Lesson 3

- Read Chapters 12–18. Discuss vocabulary words.
- Choose a vocabulary activity to complete. (page 9)
- Make a journal. (Page 16)
- Learn about snakebites. (page 17)
- Study Native American tribes. (page 18)
- Examine your agenda. (page 19)
- Administer the Section 2 Quiz. (page 15)
- Introduce the vocabulary list for Section 3. (page 8)

Lesson 4

- Read Chapters 19–24. Discuss vocabulary words.
- Choose a vocabulary activity to complete. (page 9)
- Create your soul. (page 21)
- Research Native American legends. (page 22)
- Keep a journal. (page 23)
- Explore your mother's identity. (page 24)
- Administer the Section 3 Quiz. (page 20)
- Introduce the vocabulary list for Section 4. (page 8)

Lesson 5

- Read Chapters 25–32. Discuss vocabulary words.
- Choose a vocabulary activity to complete. (page 9)
- Make your own Pandora's box. (page 26)
- Compare Mount Rushmore with Crazy Horse. (page 27)
- Study Greek mythology. (page 28)
- Examine what worries you and what gives you hope. (page 29)
- Administer Section 4 Quiz. (page 25)
- Introduce the vocabulary list for Section 5. (page 8)

Lesson 6

- Read Chapters 33–44. Discuss vocabulary words
- Choose a vocabulary activity to complete. (page 9)
- Make fortune cookies. (page 31)
- Research famous mothers. (page 32)
- Make a geyser. (page 33)
- Walk in someone else's moccasins. (page 34)
- Administer Section 5 Quiz. (page 30)

Lesson 7

- Discuss questions students have about the book. (page 35)
- Assign a book report and research activity. (pages 36–37)
- Begin work on one or more culminating activities. (pages 38–42)

Lesson 8

- Choose and administer one or more of the Unit Tests. (pages 43–45)
- Discuss students' feelings about the book.
- Provide a bibliography of related reading. (page 46)

Before the Book

Before you begin reading *Walk Two Moons* with your students, complete one or more of the following pre-reading activities to stimulate their interest and enhance comprehension.

1. Examine the cover of the book. Ask students to predict the book's plot, characters, and setting.

2. Discuss the title. Ask students what "walk two moons" might mean. See if students can predict anything from the title.

3. Pose the following questions and ask the students to respond:

   - Why might a 13-year-old girl have no mother?

   - What would it be like to move to the city when you've lived in the country your whole life?

   - How would you feel if you saw your father crying?

   - What might a road trip across the country with your grandparents be like?

   - How would you feel if your mother disappeared?

   - What are your parents like as people?

   - Can you understand someone else by imagining you are that person?

   - What and who are you afraid of?

   - What would it be like to be the only child of a single father?

   - What do you know about Native Americans in contemporary times?

4. Direct students to work in groups to brainstorm how a girl might cope with losing her mother. Have them share the ideas with the class.

5. Ask students to work in groups to list the different reasons a father might cry. Ask them to examine stereotypes about men and crying. Discuss whether they feel it is all right for men to cry and why or why not.

6. Direct students to work in groups to brainstorm what one might do if one's mother disappeared. Would you go to the police? Try to solve the mystery yourself? Ask for help from friends and family? Share the answers with the class.

7. Have students work in groups to make a list of what they know about contemporary Native Americans. Then list what they know about Native Americans in history. Compare the lists and share the findings with the class.

About the Author

Sharon Creech was born in South Euclid, Ohio—the same city Sal and her father live in after they leave Kentucky. She describes life with her sister, three brothers, and parents as "noisy and rowdy." Her house was always full of relatives. In fact, it sounds a lot like the house in which Sal's friend Mary Lou Finney grows up.

One summer, Sharon Creech took a road trip with her family. "The five-day trip out to Idaho when I was twelve had a powerful effect on me," she writes. "What a huge and amazing country! I had no idea then that thirty-some years later, I would recreate that trip in a book called *Walk Two Moons*." Creech and her family took many trips to Kentucky to visit her cousins. Sal's memories of the trees and birds and swimming holes back home are created out of Sharon Creech's own happy experiences during summer vacations.

While Creech was growing up, she wanted to be a painter, an ice skater, a teacher, a reporter, and a singer. In college, she enjoyed literature and writing courses. After graduating, she taught English to high school students in Switzerland and in England. That is how she learned so much about what makes a story work. Sharon Creech's first two books were written for adults and published in England. Then she wrote a novel for young adults, titled *Absolutely Normal Chaos*. This is a story about Mary Lou Finney and her family. Creech has been writing for middle-grade and high school students ever since.

Walk Two Moons was the first of Sharon Creech's books to be published in the United States. It won the Newbery Medal in 1995—an award which recognizes the best children's novel of the year. "No one was more surprised than I was," she writes. "I'm still a little bit in shock."

The idea for *Walk Two Moons* came out of a fortune cookie the author received. "Don't judge a man until you've walked two moons in his moccasins," her fortune read. She began thinking about Native Americans and journeys and the idea that people aren't always what they seem to be. She had an image of Sal and of the place in which she lived, and wrote the novel from these images.

Sharon Creech is married to Lyle Rig, who is the headmaster of The Pennington School in New Jersey. They have two grown children, named Rob and Karin. Creech's other books include *Chasing Redbird*, *Pleasing the Ghost*, *Bloomability*, *The Wanderer*, and *Fishing in the Air*. Some of her favorite children's writers are Katherine Paterson, Virginia Hamilton, Jerry Spinelli, Christopher Paul Curtis, and Karen Cushman. Sharon Creech herself hopes to keep writing for many more years. You can see pictures of her and learn more about her books at her Web site—*www.sharoncreech.com*.

Walk Two Moons

By Sharon Creech

(Harper Trophy, 1994)

(Available in Canada, and UK, HarperCollins Publishers; Australia, HarperCollins)

Thirteen-year old Sal finds herself living in a small house in Euclid, Ohio, with her father, far from their Kentucky farm. Her mother has vanished, and Sal is heartbroken. She hates her father's new friend, Margaret Cadaver, and she misses her old life.

Sal becomes friends with Phoebe Winterbottom, a girl who lives next door to Margaret Cadaver. Strange notes begin to appear on Phoebe's doorstep—notes which upset Phoebe's mother. On a road trip to Idaho with her grandparents, Sal tells the story of Phoebe and her mother.

Gramps and Gram agree to drive Sal along the route her own mother took when she left suddenly for Idaho. In between episodes of Phoebe's story, Sal and her grandparents have many adventures. They almost get robbed, and Gram gets bitten by a snake. They visit the Badlands, Mount Rushmore, and Yellowstone National Park before arriving in Idaho where they rush to the hospital.

During the trip, Sal tells Gramps and Gram about her strange teacher, Mr. Birkway. He makes his students write in journals, portions of which he then reads to the class, always trying to keep the author's identities unknown. In school, Sal meets Mary Lou Finney and her cousin, Ben. She notices the difference between Phoebe's very proper household and Mary Lou's chaotic family life. Ben notices Sal, and he tries to kiss her. Sal's own family life remains confusing. Her father continues to visit Margaret Cadaver, but Sal discovers him crying and looking through old photo albums at pictures of her mother.

Suddenly, Phoebe's mother disappears. Sal is reminded of her own mother's disappearance, and she promises to help Phoebe find her mother. The two girls begin looking for clues. A strange young man whom Phoebe refers to as "the lunatic" is their prime suspect. They try to enlist the help of the police, who don't take Mrs. Winterbottom's disappearance seriously. Finally, Sal and Phoebe take a trip and discover something shocking.

Walk Two Moons is a story about mothers and daughters. It explores the importance of never pre-judging a person, and it emphasizes compassion. By the end of the story, Sal learns several important truths, the most important of which is that you really can't understand a person completely—not even your own mother—until you walk two moons in her moccasins.

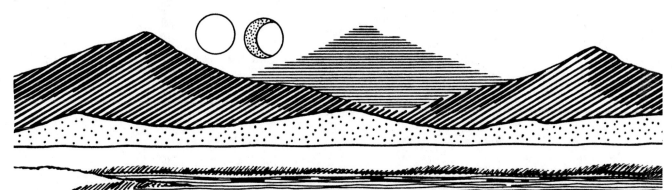

Vocabulary Lists

Below are lists of vocabulary words for each section of chapters. A variety of ideas for using this vocabulary in classroom activities is offered on page 9.

Section 1 (Chapters 1–11)

caboodle	diabolic
tottery	divulge(d)
extensive	ambush
lunatic	pandemonium
heartily	shrapnel
omnipotent	gullible
defiance	flinch
ruination	

Section 2 (Chapters 12–18)

elaborate	dramatic(ally)
rhododendron	cantankerous
detour	crotchety
manna	sullen
malevolent	alternator
skim(med)	carburetor
native	colossal
aspen grove	ornery

Section 3 (Chapters 19–24)

mere(ly)	skittish	plummet(ed)
cavort(ed)	amnesia	outcroppings
lively	farfetched	tentative(ly)
detect	blackmail	
distinctive	pitiful	
malinger	gorge (n.)	

Section 4 (Chapters 25–32)

optimistic	plagues	pious
chaotic	careen(ing)	ulcer
glum(ly)	somber(ly)	berserk
sarcastic	musty	
extensive(ly)	ghastly	
besiege(ing)	poise(d)	

Section 5 (Chapters 33–44)

slaughter	psychiatric	wean(ing)
vaporize(ing)	fidget(ed)	treacherous
ogle(ing)	agitate(d)	scour
consecutive	fiends	legitimate
percolate(ing)	quizzical	maneuver

8

Vocabulary Activity Ideas

You can help your students learn the vocabulary words in *Walk Two Moons* by providing them with the stimulating vocabulary activities below.

- Ask your students to work in groups to create an illustrated book of the vocabulary words and their meanings.

- Separate students into groups. Use the vocabulary words to create crossword puzzles and word searches. Groups can trade puzzles with each other.

- Play "Guess the Definition." One student writes down the correct definition of the vocabulary word. The others write down false definitions, close enough to the original definition that their classmates might be fooled. Read all definitions, and then challenge students to guess the correct one. The students whose definitions mislead their classmates get a point for each student fooled.

- Use the word in five different sentences. Compare sentences and discuss.

- Write a short story using as many of the words as possible. Students may then read their stories in groups.

- Encourage your students to use each new vocabulary word in a conversation five times during one day. They can take notes on how and when the word was used, and then share their experience with the class.

- Play Vocabulary Charades. Each student or group of students gets a word to act out. Other students must guess the word.

- Play Vocabulary Pictures. Each student or group of students must draw a picture representing a word on the chalkboard or on paper. Other students must guess the word.

- Challenge students to a vocabulary bee. In groups or separately, students must spell the word correctly, and give its proper definition.

- Talk about the different forms that a word may take. For instance, some words may function as nouns, as well as verbs. The word *judge* is a good example of a word which can be both a noun and a verb. Some words which look identical may have completely different meanings; in *Walk Two Moons*, the word *gorge* refers to a deep cavern in the land, but it can also be a verb which means to "eat a great deal."

- Ask your students to make flash cards with the word printed on one side and the definition printed on the other. Ask your students to work with a younger class to help them learn the definitions of the new words, using the flash cards.

- Write the words with glue on stiff paper and then cover the glue with glitter or sand. Alternatively, students may write the words on bread with a squeeze bottle full of jam, creating an edible lesson!

Quiz Time

Answer the following questions about chapters 1 through 11.

1. How is Sal's new house in Ohio different from her house in Kentucky? _____

   _____

   _____

2. Why did Gramps and Gram take Sal to Idaho? Name at least two reasons. _____

   _____

   _____

3. How did Sal get her full name? _____

   _____

   _____

4. Why does Mary Lou Finney say that Sal is brave?_____

   _____

   _____

5. What does Sal think of Phoebe's parents? _____

   _____

   _____

6. How is Mary Lou's house different from Phoebe's house? _____

   _____

   _____

7. What two messages appear on Phoebe's doorstep?_____

   _____

   _____

8. What happens to Sal every time someone touches her? Why do you think this happens? _____

   _____

   _____

Blackberry Pie

The first time Sal visits Phoebe's house, her mother makes blackberry pie for dessert. "I could not admit that blackberries reminded me of my mother," Sal says. She eats the pie, remembering the time her mother put two small dishes full of blackberries on the breakfast table, one at her father's place and one at hers.

Materials

- mixing bowls
- measuring cups and spoons
- 8" (20 cm) pie plate
- 2¼ cups (535 mL) all-purpose flour
- 1 teaspoon (5mL) salt
- ½ cup (120 mL) vegetable oil
- 3 tablespoons (45 mL) cold water
- ⅔ cup (160 mL) white sugar
- ½ teaspoon (2.5 mL) ground cinnamon
- 3 cups (720 mL) fresh blackberries

Directions

- Preheat the oven to 425° F (220° C).
- Mix together two cups of flour and salt in a mixing bowl. Make a well in the center. Pour in the oil and water. Stir briefly to form dough.
- Separate dough into two balls, using 3/4 of the dough for the first ball and the remaining dough for the second. Place a sheet of wax paper over the larger ball and roll it out. The dough may be crumbly.
- Line an eight-inch pie pan with this rolled-out dough. Pinch around the top edge.
- Roll out the second ball and set it aside.
- In a small bowl, mix together sugar, the remaining ¼ cup (60 mL) flour, and cinnamon.
- Place washed berries in a large bowl and sprinkle sugar mixture over them. Stir to coat. Spread the filling in the dough-lined pie pan.
- Cut the rolled out dough from the second ball into strips (See illustration). Lay the strips on top as shown.
- Bake the pie for 30–45 minutes, or until the crust is golden-brown, and the filling is bubbly. Enjoy!

The Braille Alphabet

Margaret Cadaver's mother, Mrs. Partridge, is blind. Still, she can tell a great deal about a person just by observing with her other four senses.

> *"Mrs. Partridge put her fingers up to Phoebe's face and mashed around gently over her eyelids and down her cheeks. 'Just as I thought. It's two eyes, a nose, and a mouth.' Mrs. Partridge laughed a wicked laugh that sounded as if it were bouncing off jagged rocks. 'You're thirteen years old.'"*
>
> —*Walk Two Moons* by Sharon Creech

Braille Facts

When Sal and Phoebe walk into Margaret Cadaver's house, they find Mrs. Partridge reading a book in Braille. In 1829, a Frenchman named Louis Braille developed an alphabet made of raised dots, enabling blind people to read by running their fingertips over the dots. Here is the Braille alphabet. Use it to write a message in Braille at the bottom of the page.

Message

Making a Map

Throughout *Walk Two Moons,* Sal tells her story about Phoebe Winterbottom to her grandparents on their road trip across the country.

> *"It was after all the adventures of Phoebe that my grandparents came up with a plan to drive from Kentucky to Ohio, where they would pick me up, and then the three of us would drive two thousand miles west to Lewiston, Idaho."*
>
> —*Walk Two Moons* by Sharon Creech

Study this map of the United States below. You will use it several times as you read *Walk Two Moons.*

A symbol is an object that represents another person, place, or thing. Your first assignment is to draw symbols on the map. Using an atlas, locate Bybanks, Kentucky, where Sal grew up (If you cannot find Bybanks on your map, locate Quincy on the south bank of the Ohio River and assume that Bybanks is just a fictional name for Quincy). Mark the location with a symbol—something that represents Sal's old life.

Now locate Euclid, Ohio. Mark its location with a symbol of Sal's new life. Draw a line from Bybanks (Quincy) to Euclid.

As you read about Sal's trip across the country with Gramps and Gram, locate the places they stop in your atlas. Mark each location on the map below with a symbol. Connect each of their stopping places with a line which will eventually end in Idaho.

Describe Your Mother

Sal knows a great deal about her mother. She knows that she prefers the term "Indian" to "Native American." She knows that her mother's name is Chanhassen and that she is descended from the Seneca Indian tribe. She remembers that her mother once left two dishes of blackberries on the breakfast table, and she knows her mother was kind and loving. What Sal doesn't know is why her mother left her to travel to Lewiston, Idaho.

What do you know about your mother? Answer the questions below.

1. What is your mother's birth name—that is, the first and last names she was born with?

   _____

2. What is your mother's nationality and ethnic and/or racial background?

   _____

3. What are your mother's parents' names?

   _____

4. Where did your mother live as a child?

   _____

5. Where did your mother go to school?

   _____

6. What was your mother's favorite book when she was in school?

   _____

7. List one thing you do not know about your mother.

   _____

8. Describe one good memory you have of your mother.

   _____

   _____

   _____

   _____

Quiz Time

Answer the following questions about chapters 12 through 18.

1. What does Sal think when she smokes the peace pipe in Pipestone, Minnesota? _____

   _____

   _____

2. Why did Gram want to know all about Gramps' dog before she married him? _____

   _____

   _____

3. How does Sal's father's behavior change when he visits Margaret Cadaver? _____

   _____

   _____

4. What trick does Sal do with a rock from the river that surprises the boy with the knife? _____

   _____

   _____

5. Why does Gram end up in the hospital? _____

   _____

   _____

6. How do Phoebe and Prudence treat their mother? _____

   _____

   _____

7. Why does Sugar decide to go on a trip to Idaho? _____

   _____

   _____

8. Why does Sal's father have to leave Bybanks, Kentucky? _____

   _____

   _____

9. What does the name Bybanks suggest to you about the town's location? Can you think of an
   explanation for why you may not have been able to locate this town on the map? _____

   _____

   _____

Making a Journal

When Sal arrives at her new school, she meets an unusual English teacher who asks her to write in a journal.

> *"Midway through the first class, Mr. Birkway asked for everyone's summer journals. He flung himself up and down the aisles, receiving the journals as if they were manna from heaven. 'Wonderful,' he said to each journal-giver.*
>
> *I was worried. I had no journal."*
>
> —*Walk Two Moons* by Sharon Creech

A journal can be a place in which to record your most private thoughts. Or it can be a place in which you describe scenery, people, or funny events. No matter what you use it for, your journal shows your individuality and creativity.

Materials

- paper—approximately 20 sheets, measuring 8 ½" x 11" (21 cm x 27.5 cm), lined or blank
- two sheets of 8 ½" x 11" (21 cm x 27.5 cm) cardboard-backed, vinyl-covered paper
- yarn

- hole punch
- old magazines
- glue
- glitter
- stickers

Directions

1. Punch two holes in the vinyl-covered front cover sheet, ½" (1 cm) from the left edge and 2" (5 cm) down from the top and bottom edges. Use this cover sheet as a stencil to mark the location of the holes on the 20 sheets of paper, as well as the back cover.

2. Punch holes in the paper and back cover. Thread the yarn through the holes, threading in and out a few times so that your bookbinding is strong. Tie a bow on the front cover.

3. Decorate the front of your journal with pictures that symbolize your life. Use cutout pictures from magazines, glitter, and stickers to personalize your journal.

4. On the inside front page of your journal, copy the following list and complete the spaces with the appropriate information:

- My Name: _____
- My Age: _____
- My Grade: _____
- My School:_____
- My Favorite Book:_____
- My Favorite Color: _____
- My Favorite Song: _____
- My Favorite Movie: _____
- My Favorite Food: _____

Snakebite!

In South Dakota, Gramps and Gram take a detour to swim in the Missouri River. There, Gram gets bitten by a water moccasin. This is just one type of poisonous snake in the United States.

In groups of four, choose one of the snakes listed below to research. (Each group should choose a different snake.) Using an encyclopedia, books, or the Internet, answer the questions below about your chosen snake. Draw a picture of the snake. Then share the information with the rest of the class.

- *Eastern Diamondback Rattlesnake*
- *Western Diamondback Rattlesnake*
- *Sidewinder*
- *Copperhead*
- *Cotton Mouth* (another name for *water moccasin*)
- *Coral Snake*

1. What snake did you choose? _____

2. Where does this snake live?_____

3. How long is this adult snake? _____

4. How poisonous is this snake? _____

5. Draw a picture of this snake here. Color it, if possible.

My Snake

The boy with the knife drops Gramps' wallet and begins sucking the snake's venom out of Grams' leg. In your group, research the proper way to treat a snake bite. List the steps below. Share your findings with the class.

How to Treat a Snakebite

Native American Tribes

Sal's mother is a descendent of the Seneca Indian tribe. Before Europeans came to America, Native American tribes lived here. There are still many different tribes of Native Americans in existence today.

Using an encyclopedia, books, or the Internet, research the Native American tribe that lived nearby (and perhaps still lives) where your city is today. Answer the following questions.

1. What is the name of the tribe?_____

2. What type of houses did this tribe live in? _____

3. What type of foods did this tribe eat? _____

   _____

4. Describe this tribe's methods of transportation. _____

   _____

   _____

5. Describe this tribe's particular styles of dance and/or music and celebrations. _____

   _____

   _____

   _____

6. What language did this tribe speak? _____

7. Did this tribe disappear? If so, when and why did they disappear?_____

   _____

8. Are members of this tribe still alive in your area? If so, what are the names of two of the members? _____

Now, research the names of the different tribes that lived in the states Sal and her grandparents travel through. If you choose to use the Internet in your research, you might click on one of the following search engines: *www.google.com*   *www.yahoo.com*   *www.netscape.com*

Write the names of the different tribes below and in the appropriate states on an enlargement of the map on page 13.

_____

_____

What Is Your Agenda?

> *"As we left Phoebe's house, there on the front steps was another white envelope with a blue sheet of paper inside. The message was: Everyone has his own agenda."*
>
> —*Walk Two Moons* by Sharon Creech

An agenda is a plan or an outline. The note Phoebe finds means that everyone has a plan for his or her life. What is your agenda? Answer the questions below to find out.

1. What do you hope to accomplish by the end of this year? _____

   _____

   _____

2. What makes you happy? _____

   _____

   _____

3. What makes you angry? _____

   _____

   _____

4. What do you want to be when you grow up? Why? _____

   _____

   _____

5. What do you plan on doing after you finish high school? _____

   _____

   _____

6. Where would you most like to live? Why? _____

   _____

   _____

7. What means the most to you? _____

   _____

   _____

8. What one thing would you like to accomplish in your life? _____

   _____

   _____

Quiz Time

Answer the following questions about chapters 19 throught 24.

1. What message appears on the doorstep after Phoebe's mother disappears? _____

_____

_____

2. Why does Mr. Birkway remind Sal of her mother? _____

_____

_____

3. What is Sal's mother's blackberry kiss? _____

_____

_____

4. What photo is Sal's father looking at when she discovers him sitting over the photo album?

_____

_____

5. What does Sal's soul look like?_____

_____

_____

6. What happens to Sal's house when her mother leaves? _____

_____

_____

7. Why does Phoebe's father doubt that his wife has been kidnapped? _____

_____

_____

8. What happened to Sal's mother's new baby? _____

_____

_____

Creating Your Soul

> *"Mr. Birkway gave us a fifteen-second exercise. As fast as we could, without thinking, we were to draw something. He would tell us what we were to draw when everyone was ready. 'Remember,' he said. 'Don't think. Just draw. Fifteen seconds. Ready? Draw your soul. Go.'"*
>
> —*Walk Two Moons* by Sharon Creech

What is a *soul*? The dictionary says that a soul is a person's essence—that which makes a person unique. The soul is invisible, but you can, as Sal did, create an image of what yours might look like.

Materials

- heavy white cardboard, one piece for each student
- glue
- scissors
- old magazines and greeting cards
- glitter
- pens and crayons

- yarn
- watercolor paints
- buttons
- stickers
- scraps of fabric and colored paper

Draw a sketch of your soul in the frame below. Working from your rough draft, use the craft materials to make a final picture of your soul on a piece of cardboard. Hang your picture in the classroom.

Native American Legends

A legend is a story passed down from generation to generation. Often, it teaches a valuable lesson. Sal's mother once told her the story of Napi, the Old Man who created men and women, according to the Blackfoot Indian tribe.

"To decide if these new people should live forever or die, Napi selected a stone. 'If the stone floats,' he said, 'you will live forever. If it sinks, you will die.' Napi dropped the stone into the water. It sank. People die."

—*Walk Two Moons* by Sharon Creech

Divide into groups of three students each. Using library books or the Internet, choose three Native American legends to study. Read them and then copy the form below to answer the questions for each legend.

Native American Legend

1. Title:

2. Native American tribe:

3. Main character:

4. Summary of what happens in the story:

5. The lesson this story teaches:

Now that you've studied three Native American legends, come up with one of your own. Select one person in your group to write your story down, one to check for spelling and grammar, and one to read your legend to the class.

Keeping a Journal

Mr. Birkway asks his students to keep a journal. He causes a great deal of trouble among the students when he reads parts of their journals out loud to the class. Traditionally, journals are used to record someone's private thoughts. They should be read only with the consent of the writer.

Phoebe is going through a difficult time. Outwardly, she behaves in an obnoxious manner to her friends, including Sal. But Sal suspects Phoebe is hurting inside because of the disappearance of her mother. For a few minutes, try to walk in Phoebe's "moccasins." Below, write a journal entry like the one you think she might write. Try to fill her entire page.

Phoebe's Journal

_____

_____

_____

_____

_____

_____

_____

_____

_____

On page 16, you learned to make your own journal. Now that it is completed, you may write in it. Begin by answering the questions below. Try to answer one each day for the entire school week, writing at least a page every time.

- Who is your best friend? What are your feelings about him or her?

- What do you love to do and why?

- What do you think of school? Which classes are your favorites? Which ones do you dislike?

- Are you happy with your life? Why or why not? How could you change it to make it better?

- What is your opinion about writing? Do you love it? Hate it? Why?

Underneath It All

Sal's mother goes on a trip to Idaho in an effort to remember who she really is. Sal is confused by this.

> *"Later I learned that she had a cousin in Lewiston, Idaho. 'I haven't seen her for fifteen years,' my mother said, 'and that's good because she'll tell me what I'm really like.'*
>
> *'I could tell you that, Sugar,' my father said.*
>
> *'No, I mean before I was a wife and a mother. I mean **underneath**, where I am Chanhassen.'"*
>
> —*Walk Two Moons* by Sharon Creech

On page 14, you wrote a description of your mother. But who is she underneath? Interview your mother again and ask her the following questions. Write the answers below.

1. What makes you happy? _____

   _____

2. What makes you sad? _____

   _____

3. What makes you angry? _____

   _____

4. What is your favorite thing to do?_____

   _____

5. What do you really dislike doing?_____

   _____

6. What are you afraid of? _____

   _____

7. What did you want to be when you were growing up?_____

   _____

8. Remember question number 8 from page 14—List one thing you don't know about your mother? Find out now!_____

   _____

Quiz Time

Answer the following questions about chapters 25 through 32.

1. Why do you think Sal invites Phoebe to spend the night? _____

   _____

   _____

2. What does Sal notice about dinner with the Finney family? _____

   _____

   _____

3. Why doesn't Sal comfort Phoebe when she's crying? _____

   _____

   _____

4. How does Sal learn to drive?_____

   _____

   _____

5. Why does the poem "The Tide Rises, the Tide Falls" scare Sal?_____

   _____

   _____

6. What items does Phoebe show Sergeant Bickle? _____

   _____

   _____

7. How does Mrs. Partridge know that Phoebe and Sal are in her house? _____

   _____

   _____

8. How do the students react when Mr. Birkway reads parts of their journals out loud in class? _____

   _____

   _____

Pandora's Box

Phoebe tells Mr. Birkway's class the story of Pandora and the gifts given to her by the gods.

> *"Last, there was a beautiful box, covered in gold and jewels, and this is very important—she was forbidden to open the box."*
>
> —*Walk Two Moons* by Sharon Creech

Pandora's box was full of bad things. In fact, the only good thing it contained was *hope*. But you may choose to use your box to hold good things, if you wish.

Materials

- one small box for each student
- white glue
- paintbrushes
- old magazines and catalogs
- scissors

Directions

First, cut out pictures from magazines and catalogs to decorate your box. These might be pictures that illustrate your feelings about the world. You might choose to find pictures that show how you feel about your mother, your home, or a friend.

Now, begin gluing the pictures to the outside of your box, overlapping them to make a collage. Try to cover the box completely but make sure to leave enough space so that you can lift the lid. Allow the glue to dry.

Finally, paint a thin layer of glue over the pictures. Allow to dry. Repeat. Your box will now have the shiny look of shellac, and it will be resistant to dirt and ripping.

You may choose to take a walking tour of your school's neighborhood in order to collect materials for your box. Perhaps you will include acorns, leaves, and rocks. Or perhaps you will put in a found penny, a broken bracelet, or an interesting discovery of another sort. The choice is yours!

Mount Rushmore and Crazy Horse

Gram, Gramps, and Sal visit Mount Rushmore in the Black Hills of South Dakota on their way to Idaho. Sal sees the sixty-foot-tall faces of four presidents and thinks the following:

> *"It was fine seeing the presidents, I've got nothing against the presidents, but you'd think the Sioux would be mighty sad to have those white faces carved into their sacred hill. I bet my mother was upset. I wondered why whoever carved them couldn't have put a couple Indians up there, too."*
>
> —*Walk Two Moons* by Sharon Creech

Possibly, Sal and her grandparents didn't know about another stone monument in the Black Hills, a monument called Crazy Horse.

Get into groups of four, and then pair up. Each pair should choose to research either Mount Rushmore or Crazy Horse, using books or the Internet.

Here are two Web sites you may use in your research:

- Mount Rushmore
  http://www.travelsd.com/parks/rushmore/

- Crazy Horse
  http://www.crazyhorse.org/

Answer the questions below for your particular monument and draw a picture of it. Then compare your answers with those of the others in your group. What are the similarities between the two monuments? What are the differences? (Use the back of the page if you need more room.)

1. Name of your monument? _____

2. Who carved your monument? _____

3. When was your monument started? When was it finished?_____

4. Who is depicted on your monument? _____

5. Where is your monument located? _____

6. What other places might you visit near your monument?_____

7. List two interesting facts about your monument. _____

8. Draw a picture of your monument in the space below.

Greek Gods and Goddesses

Myths are similar to legends in that they are stories about people who may or may not have existed. They help to explain something or teach a lesson. In chapter 27 of *Walk Two Moons*, Phoebe gives an oral report on the myth of Pandora's box. Previously, Ben gave a report on the Greek god Prometheus.

Study the list of Greek gods and goddesses on the chart below. Using an encyclopedia, books, or the Internet, fill in the blanks on the chart. The first one has been done for you.

God/Goddess	Best Known For
Prometheus	He stole fire from the heavens and gave it to man.
Aphrodite	
Apollo	
Ares	
Artemis	
Athena	
Demeter	
Dionysius	
Hades	
Hephaestus	
Hera	
Hermes	
Hestia	
Persephone	
Poseidon	
Zeus	

What Worries You?
What Gives You Hope?

Sal thinks for a long time about the story of Pandora's box. She considers all the things she worries about, and then reflects on the power of hope.

> *"I wondered why someone would put a good thing such as Hope in a box with sickness and kidnapping and murder. It was fortunate that it was there, though. If not, people would have the birds of sadness nesting in their hair all the time, because of nuclear war and the greenhouse effect and bombs and stabbings and lunatics."*
>
> —*Walk Two Moons* by Sharon Creech

Answer the questions below. Then, choose one to expand on in your journal. Try to fill one page.

1. What are you afraid of? Why? _____

   _____

2. What makes you nervous? Why? _____

   _____

3. Name one thing in the newspaper or on the news that concerns you. Why are you worried about this particular thing? _____

   _____

4. Imagine the worst thing that could happen to you. What is it? _____

   _____

5. What cheers you up when you're feeling scared or worried?_____

   _____

6. Who helps you to feel better when you've been upset? What does this person do to help?_____

   _____

7. What gives you hope? _____

   _____

8. What might you do to give other people hope? _____

   _____

Quiz Time

Answer the following questions about Chapters 33 through 44.

1. What does Mr. Birkway reveal about Mrs. Cadaver? _____

   _____

   _____

2. Why does Grams cry? _____

   _____

   _____

3. What does Mr. Birkway apologize for? How do you feel about this?_____

   _____

   _____

4. What do Phoebe and Sal see on the college campus that shocks them?_____

   _____

   _____

5. What does Sal find out about Ben's mother? _____

   _____

   _____

6. What does Mrs. Winterbottom reveal about the young man she's been seeing? _____

   _____

   _____

7. Why does Grams end up in the hospital? _____

   _____

   _____

8. Why doesn't Sal's mother ever come back to her? _____

   _____

   _____

Fortune Cookies

Near the end of *Walk Two Moons,* Sal discovers who has been leaving the mysterious notes on Phoebe's doorstep. The person responsible for the notes says:

> *"'I thought they would be grandiful surprises for you—like fortune cookies, only I didn't have any cookies to put them in. Did you like them anyway?'"*
>
> —*Walk Two Moons* by Sharon Creech

Materials (*makes 30*)

- 10 tablespoons (150 mL) unsalted butter
- 8 egg whites
- 2 cups (450 g) superfine sugar
- 1 cup (225 g) sifted all-purpose flour
- pinch of salt
- 6 tablespoons (90 mL) heavy cream
- 2 teaspoons (10 mL) almond extract
- nonstick cooking spray

- baking sheets
- saucepan
- mixing bowl
- clean dishtowel
- spatula
- fortune strip from the bottom of this page.
- beater
- measuring spoons

Directions

Preheat oven to 400° F (200° C). Spray two cookie sheets with cooking spray. Melt butter in saucepan over low heat and set aside.

Combine egg whites and sugar. Beat on medium speed for 30 seconds. Add flour and salt; beat until combined. Add butter, cream, and extract and beat about 30 seconds.

Pour 1 tablespoon of batter onto half the baking sheet and spread with the back of a spoon into a thin five-inch circle. Repeat on the other half of the sheet. Bake until the edges of the cookies turn golden, about eight minutes.

Now, slide a spatula under one cookie and place it on a kitchen towel. Using fingers, fold the cookie in half, pinching the top together to form a semicircle. Hold the cookie with a finger inserted into each open end. Press into the center of the cookie while bending the two open ends together and down to form the shape of a fortune cookie. *Note:* Once the cookie hardens (almost immediately), you cannot fold it. Finally, thread your fortunes through the cookies. Put them on a plate and offer one to each student. Compare fortunes!

Mrs. Partridge wrote words of wisdom on the "fortunes" she left on Phoebe's doorstep. Think of some wise words that are all your own. Write them on the strip below, then cut out the strip and put it in a fortune cookie.

Famous Mothers

Walk Two Moons is a book about mothers. In it, readers follow the adventures of Sal's mother and Phoebe's mother. Mothers are also people. Often, they hold down jobs, play sports, and champion social causes, as well as raising their children. Working in groups of three, use books, encyclopedias, or the Internet to research the famous mothers below. Fill out the following chart. The first one has been done for you.

Famous Mother	Children	Accomplishments
Queen Victoria	Four sons and five daughters	Reigned over England until her death in 1901. Was influential in foreign affairs and setting social standards.
Coretta Scott King		
Laura Ingalls Wilder		
Florence Griffith Joyner		
Marie Curie		
Mary Wolstonecraft		
Eleanor Roosevelt		
Wilma Mankiller		
Abigail Adams		
Margaret Mead		
Madeleine L'Engle		
Toni Morrison		

Yellowstone and Old Faithful

Gram, Gramps, and Sal visit Yellowstone National Park, where they see the geyser known as Old Faithful.

> *"More steam, boiling and hissing, and a huge jing-bang spray of water surged out, climbing and climbing, and then more and more, until it looked like a whole river of water was shooting straight up into the air.*
>
> *"'It looks like an upsidey-down waterfall!' Gram said."*
>
> —*Walk Two Moons* by Sharon Creech

A geyser occurs when underground water in a cavern comes in contact with rocks which have been heated by volcanic activity. Steam builds inside the cavern until it gushes, with water, out of a hole on the ground's surface.

Facts About Old Faithful

- Old Faithful does not erupt every hour, but it does erupt 18 to 21 times every day.

- The column usually reaches a maximum height of 106 to 184 feet (32 m to 56 m) in 15 to 20 seconds

- Old Faithful discharges up to 7,500 gallons (285,000 L or 60,000 Imperial gallons) of water at each eruption.

- The duration of eruptions varies from 1.5 to 5.5 minutes.

- The temperature of the water at the vent is approximately 204° F (91° C).

Activity

Using information available on the Internet or other resources, select one of the following topics on which to prepare a report:

- Yellowstone Wildlife (*wolves, bears, elk, bison, etc.*)

- Wild Fire in Yellowstone

- A Ranger's Life

- History of Yellowstone

- Fishing in Yellowstone

- Map of Yellowstone Park (*Draw this instead of writing a report.*)

Walk in Someone Else's Moccasins

By the end of *Walk Two Moons*, Sal understands a great deal about her mother. Perhaps her trip to Idaho is Sal's way of walking in her mother's moccasins. Think of someone whom you do not understand well. This may be a person who confuses you—even a person you dislike. Answer the following questions below in an effort to walk in this person's moccasins. You may choose to write further on this subject in your journal.

1. What does this person do and/or say that confuses you? _____

    _____

    _____

2. What particular challenges has this person had to face?_____

    _____

    _____

3. What might this person be afraid of? _____

    _____

    _____

4. What makes this person angry?_____

    _____

    _____

5. What makes this person happy? _____

    _____

    _____

6. Why does this person act the way he or she does? _____

    _____

    _____

7. How would you act if you were this person? _____

    _____

    _____

8. What else can you do to understand this person better? _____

    _____

    _____

Any Questions?

When you finished reading *Walk Two Moons*, did you have questions that were left unanswered? Write some of your questions here.

_____

_____

_____

_____

_____

Work in groups or by yourself to predict possible answers for some or all of the questions you have asked above, as well as those written below. When you have finished, share your predictions with your class.

- Does Phoebe become friends with her new half-brother?

- Does Sal marry Ben?

- Does Sal stay on the farm forever, or does she eventually travel?

- Does Sal's father marry Mrs. Cadaver?

- Does Tom Fleet, the boy who helped Gram when she was bitten, ever come to Kentucky to visit Sal?

- Does Gloria eventually return and try to talk Gramps into marrying her?

- Do Sal and Phoebe remain friends, even though they live far from each other now?

- How does Mrs. Winterbottom's behavior change now that she's been gone for a while?

- How does Mr. Winterbottom's behavior change toward his wife?

- How do Phoebe and her sister Prudence change in their behavior toward their mother after she returns?

- Does Mrs. Partridge begin leaving notes on other people's doorsteps?

- Does Mr. Birkway ask his next year's class to keep journals, and if so, does he read them out loud?

- Does Sal ever travel to Idaho again?

- What does Sal choose as a career when she grows up?

- What career does Ben choose?

- Does Mike, Phoebe's half-brother, move in with the Winterbottoms?

- What happens to Ben's mother? Does she remain in the hospital, or does she return home?

Book Report Ideas

There are several ways to report on a book after you have read it. When you have finished *Walk Two Moons,* choose a method of reporting from the list below or come up with your own idea on how best to report on this book.

- **Make a Book Jacket**

  Design a book jacket for this book. On the front, draw a picture that you feel best captures this story. On the back, write a paragraph or two which summarizes the main points of this book.

- **Make a Time Line**

  On paper, create a time line to show the significant events in Sal's life. You may illustrate your time line, if you wish.

- **Design a Scrapbook**

  Use magazine pictures, photographs, and other illustrations to create a scrapbook that Sal might keep to document her life after her mother leaves. She might choose to decorate her scrapbook with stickers or to include a letter to her mother. She might also include pictures of her new friends and a page out of her journal.

- **Make a Collage**

  Using old magazines and photographs, design a collage that illustrates all of Sal's adventures in *Walk Two Moons*.

- **Create a Time Capsule**

  What items might Sal put in a time capsule by which to remember her time in Ohio or her trip out to Idaho with her grandparents? What container might she use as a time capsule?

- **Write a Biography**

  Do research to find out about the life of Sharon Creech. Write a biography, showing how Ms. Creech's experiences might have influenced her novel.

- **Act Out a Play**

  With one or two other students, write a play featuring some of the characters in this novel. Then act out your play for your class.

- **Design a Diorama**

  Using a shoebox as a frame, create a diorama that illustrates an important scene in the novel. You may use all sorts of materials (paper, sand, clay, paint, fabric, etc.) to bring this scene to life.

- **Make Puppets**

  Using a variety of materials, design puppets to represent one or all of the characters in this novel. You may decide to work with other students to write and perform a puppet show.

Research Ideas

As you read *Walk Two Moons*, you discovered geographic locations, events, and people about which you might wish to know more. To increase your understanding of the characters, places, and events in this novel, do research to find additional information.

Work alone or in groups to find out about one or more of the items listed below. You may use books, magazines, encyclopedias, and the Internet. Afterwards, share your findings with the class.

- Kentucky
- Euclid, Ohio
- Mount Rushmore
- Yellowstone National Park
- The Black Hills
- Seneca Native American tribe
- water moccasins
- journal writing
- blindness and Braille
- Greek myths
- Native American legends
- Newbery Award
- cholesterol
- the poet Henry Wadsworth Longfellow
- the poet e.e. cummings
- geysers
- detectives
- psychiatric wards
- strokes
- how to drive
- single parenting
- Pipestone National Monument
- Native American dancing
- World War II
- automobile accidents
- trees
- stillborn babies
- psychological stages of grief

Field Trips and Class Visits

Now that your students have learned about Native Americans, mythology, and poetry, they may enjoy taking one or more field trips related to those subjects. In addition, guests may visit your class. Choose an activity from the list below and locate the appropriate person in the phone book. Be sure to call at least two weeks in advance to give the staff plenty of time to prepare for the visit.

- **Local Native Americans**

  Locate Native Americans in your community. You may invite someone to speak and share legends in your classroom, or your town may offer a Native American education center of some sort.

- **Natural History Museum**

  Sal is attuned to the landscape of her home in Kentucky. Teach your students all about their own landscape and history with a visit to a local natural history museum. Or invite the museum's director to talk about history and nature in your classroom.

- **Poets in the Schools**

  Mr. Birkway would certainly take advantage of the nationwide program known as Poets in the Schools. Contact your local chapter to see which local poets are available to visit your classroom.

- **Poetry Readings**

  Many coffeehouses, colleges, and bookstores offer weekly poetry readings. Locate one, and treat your students to an afternoon or evening of poetry. Many of these events allow beginning poets to stand up and read, as well!

- **Psychologists**

  Students may have questions as to why Sal's and Phoebe's mothers disappear. They may wonder why Ben's mother lives in a psychiatric unit. A psychologist who agrees to visit your classroom may also explain the stages of grief one goes through after a death.

- **Retirement Home**

  Many women in retirement homes are mothers who see their daughters little, or not at all. Students will receive as much as they give when they take a trip to a local retirement home to talk with the residents. Perhaps the women there will be as interesting as Sal's grandmother!

- **Parents Without Partners**

  This national organization serving single parents and their children has chapters all over the United States. Click on *www.parentswithoutpartners.org* to locate a guest speaker who can educate your students as to the particular issues and challenges of being a single parent.

- **Native American Powwow**

  Many Native American groups hold annual or semi-annual powwows which are open to the public. There, students may sample Native American foods, look at tools and crafts, and watch traditional dancing.

In Honor of Mother

Why not invite everyone's mother (including step-mothers, foster mothers, and grandmothers) to your classroom for a party? Then each mother will know just how special she is.

Your students will enjoy planning, preparing for, and participating in their party.

Party Checklist

Three weeks before the party . . .

- Decide when and where the party will occur.

- Think of a theme for the party. Themes related to *Walk Two Moons* include Native Americans, mythology, and traveling across the United States. Your class may opt for non-book related themes such as a holiday party or one to celebrate a season or school event. Whichever theme you choose, make sure you incorporate the theme of mothers into the party.

- Talk about whom you want to invite. Explain to the class that some students may have a stepmother, foster mother, grandmother, or other female care provider that they wish to invite. Make and send the invitations on page 40.

- Discuss decorations. Will you put students' poetry up on the walls, draw pictures of each mother, or use traditional streamers and balloons?

Two weeks before the party . . .

- Decide what food and drink you will make as a class. This book provides recipes for blackberry pie and fortune cookies. Make a grocery list.

- Pass around a sign-up sheet. Each student should be encouraged to bring something unique to the party. They might bring food, sign up to play musical instruments, or show off a skill such as juggling or gymnastics.

- Send home a note to students' parents to remind them of the party, and to let them know what the student signed up to bring.

One week before the party . . .

- Send home a note reminding students of what they are to bring for the party.

- Buy and/or make decorations, including name cards on page 41.

The day before the party . . .

- Make fortune cookies and blackberry pie.

The day of the party . . .

- Place the name cards on the tables and decorate the party space.

Enjoy!

In Honor of Mother *(cont.)*

Come to a Party for You!

Day: _____

Time: _____

Place: _____

Hosts: _____

Theme: _____

Name Cards

Using the information you learned about your mother from pages 14 and 24, fill out the name card below. Fold it over on the dotted line, color in decorations, and use it to mark your mother's seat in your classroom the day of the party.

- -

My Mother's Full Name:_____

Where She Lived as a Child:_____

_____

What Makes Her Happy: _____

_____

_____

What Her Favorite Pastime Is: _____

_____

What I Like Best About my Mother: _____

_____

Write to the Author

Sharon Creech loves to get mail from her readers. She will even write you a letter in return!

Materials

- pen
- paper
- two envelopes
- two stamps
- a photo of you (optional)

First, study the sample letter below. Note where to put the date and how to begin and end your letter.

May 14, 2003

Dear Sharon Creech,

Thank you for writing Walk Two Moons. Your book made me think about my mother in a completely new way. I really enjoyed the part in the book where Sal realizes how important it is to be kind to her mother.

I am in sixth grade, and I think I would like to be a writer when I get older, just like you.

Sincerely,

Amy Smith

Now, write your letter. Think of what you enjoyed most about *Walk Two Moons*. You may want to tell Sharon a little about yourself, as well. Don't forget to include the date and a signature.

Address the first envelope with the following:

> Sharon Creech
>
> c/o HarperCollins Children's Books
>
> Author Mail
>
> 1350 Avenue of the Americas
>
> New York, New York 10019

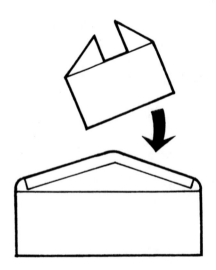

If you would like Sharon to reply to your letter, enclose a self-addressed, stamped envelope. Write your own address on the second envelope and stamp it. Fold it into thirds, as shown. Tuck it into Sharon's envelope with your letter, and mail.

She'll be glad to hear from you!

Objective Test and Essay

Matching: Match the description of each character with his or her name.

_____ 1. Sal

_____ 2. Phoebe

_____ 3. Mrs. Winterbottom

_____ 4. Mrs. Cadaver

_____ 5. Ben

_____ 6. Mr. Birkway

_____ 7. Sal's father

_____ 8. Gram

_____ 9. Gramps

_____ 10. Sal's mother

a. has to move away from Kentucky because his wife's memory is haunting him

b. survived a terrible bus accident

c. draws pictures and visits his mother in the hospital

d. leaves her family to get to know her long-lost son

e. gets bitten by a snake and has a stroke

f. travels across country after she loses her baby

g. goes to see the police after her mother disappears

h. takes a trip with her grandparents across the country

i. adopts a dog after his wife passes away

j. teaches poetry and asks his class to keep journals

True or False: Answer true or false in the blanks below.

1. _____ For a long time, Sal believes her mother might return.

2. _____ Phoebe's mother leaves her family to take a trip across the country.

3. _____ Mrs. Cadaver is a dangerous person.

4. _____ Sal and her father remain in Ohio until Sal graduates from high school.

5. _____ Sal's father is not upset about his wife's leaving.

Short Answer: On a separate sheet of paper, write a brief response to each question, using complete sentences.

1. Why does Sal's mother leave?

2. Why does Phoebe's mother leave?

3. Why does Sal's father move with her to Euclid, Ohio?

4. Why does Sal take a trip across the country with her grandparents?

Essay: Respond to the following on a separate sheet of paper.

Sal learns the value of "walking in someone else's moccasins" by the end of *Walk Two Moons*. What does it mean to "walk in someone's moccasins"? Whose moccasins does Sal walk in, and how does this help her understand that person, or people?

Response

On a separate sheet of paper, explain and respond to the following quotations as selected by your teacher.

Chapter One: "Not long ago, when I was locked in a car with my grandparents for six days, I told them the story of Phoebe, and when I finished telling them—or maybe even as I was telling them—I realized that the story of Phoebe was like the plaster wall in our old house in Bybanks, Kentucky.

Chapter Three: "As we were leaving, Margaret whispered to my father, 'John, have you told her yet—how we met?' "

Chapter Four: "The truth is, I do not have allergies, but I could not admit that blackberries reminded me of my mother."

Chapter Seven: "My mother had been there. The bus that she took out to Lewiston stopped in all the tourist spots. We were following along in her footsteps."

Chapter Eleven: " 'Dad—what do you think it means if someone touches someone else and the person being touched flinches? Do you think it means that the person being touched is getting too stiff?' "

Chapter Twelve: " 'Well, this ain't our marriage bed, but it will do.' "

Chapter Fifteen: " 'It's a water moccasin, isn't it?' she said. 'It's a poisonous one, isn't it?' "

Chapter Eighteen: " 'We have to leave because your mother is haunting me day and night. She's in the fields, the air, the barn, the walls, the trees.' "

Chapter Twenty-one: " The duplicate designs were: a circle with a large maple leaf in the center, the tips of the leaf touching the sides of the circle. One of the maple leaf circles was mine. The other was Ben's."

Chapter Twenty-two: " 'A person isn't a bird. You can't cage a person.' "

Chapter Twenty-four: "Sometimes you know in your heart you love someone, but you have to go away before your head can figure it out."

Chapter Twenty-six: "I felt bad for Phoebe. I knew I should get up and try to be nice, but I remembered when I had felt like that, and I knew that sometimes you just wanted to be alone with the birds of sadness."

Chapter Thirty: " 'I just knew,' she said. 'Your shoes make a particular sound and you have a particular smell.' "

Chapter Thirty-one: "I recognized the son. It was the lunatic."

Chapter Forty-two: " 'A bus went off the road here—a year or more ago,' he said."

Conversations

Work in groups according to the numbers in parentheses to write or act out the conversations that might have occurred in *Walk Two Moons*.

• Phoebe and her half-brother, Mike, have a conversation about their mother. (*2 people*)

• Margaret Cadaver and Sal talk about Sal's mother. (*2 people*)

• Mr. Birkway talks to his sister, Margaret Cadaver, about what he read in Sal's and Phoebe's journals. (*2 people*)

• Sal, Ben, and Mary Lou discuss Phoebe's strange behavior. (*3 people*)

• Sal and Phoebe go over to visit Mrs. Partridge. (*3 people*)

• Margaret Cadaver and Sal's father speak for the first time on the telephone, after the accident. (*2 people*)

• Ben tells Sal how he feels about her. (*2 people*)

• Gramps tells Sal how he feels about Gram's death. (*2 people*)

• Phoebe, Prudence, and Mr. Winterbottom discuss how they can better behave toward Mrs. Winterbottom. (*3 people*)

• Mr. Winterbottom and Sergeant Bickle talk about Mrs. Winterbottom's disappearance. (*2 people*)

• Mrs. Winterbottom and Mike talk for the first time since she gave him up for adoption. (*2 people*)

• Phoebe, Mary Lou, and Ben plan a going-away party for Sal. (*3 people*)

• Ben and Phoebe visit Sal in Kentucky. (*3 people*)

• Margaret Cadaver and Sal's mother talk about their families on the bus trip across country. (*2 people*)

• Mrs. Winterbottom tells Phoebe why she was so terrified when her son found her. (*2 people*)

• Ben tells Sal why his mother is in a psychiatric unit. (*2 people*)

• Gram and Gramps talk about why they are going to take Sal across the country to Idaho. (*2 people*)

Bibliography of Related Reading

Fiction

Carter, Forrest. *The Education of Little Tree.* (University of New Mexico Press, 1976)

Creech, Sharon. *Absolutely Normal Chaos.* (HarperCollins, 1997)

Curtis, Christopher Paul. *Bud, Not Buddy.* (Delacorte, 1999)

DiCamillo, Kate. *Because of Winn-Dixie.* (Candlewick, 2001)

Dorris, Michael. *A Yellow Raft in Blue Water.* (Henry Holt, 1987)

Hart, Melissa. *Long Way Home.* (Windstorm Creative, 2003)

MacLachlan, Patricia. *Sarah, Plain and Tall.* (Harpercollins, 1985)

O'Dell, Scott. *Island of the Blue Dolphins.* (Houghton Mifflin, 1960)

Paterson, Katherine. *Bridge to Terabithia.* (HarperCollins, 1982)

Peck, Richard. *A Long Way from Chicago.* (Dell, 1998)

Peck, Richard. *A Year Down Yonder.* (Dial, 2000)

Sachar, Louis. *Holes.* (Farrar Straus & Giroux, 1998)

Salat, Christina. *Living in Secret.* (Yearling, 1994)

Poetry

cummings, e.e. *One-Hundred Selected Poems.* (Grove Press, 1989)

Longfellow, Henry Wadsworth. *Poetry for Young People.* (Sterling Publications, 1998)

Paschen, Elise and Rebekah Presson Mosby, eds. *Poetry Speaks.* (book with c.d.) (Sourcebooks Trade, 2001)

Nonfiction

Erdoes, Richard and Alfonso Ortiz, eds. *American Indian Myths and Legends.* (Pantheon Books, 1985)

Evslin, Bernard. *Heroes, Gods, and Monsters of Greek Myths.* (Bantam Young Readers, 1984)

Freedman, Russell. *The Life and Death of Crazy Horse.* (Holiday House, 1996)

Answer Key

Page 10

1. Sal's new house is small. The trees are tiny, and she misses the big trees, vast farmland, and animals she left behind in Kentucky.
2. Gramps and Gram take Sal to Idaho because they want to see the country, and they want her to see her mother.
3. Sal's parents think that the Indian tribe to which her grandmother belonged was the "Salamanca" tribe. They name her Salamanca Tree Hiddle. The tree stands for itself.
4. Mary Lou thinks Sal is brave because she cupped a spider in her hands and put it outside.
5. Sal thinks Phoebe's parents are stiff and respectable.
6. Mary Lou's house is informal, loud, and exciting compared to Phoebe's quiet, tense household.
7. "Don't judge a man until you've walked two moons in his moccasins." "Everyone has his own agenda."
8. Sal flinches whenever someone touches her. Students may remember that she hasn't been hugged for a long time, or perhaps she's angry about moving, or hurting inside.

Page 13

By the time students are finished with the book, they should have marked the following on their maps: Bybanks (Quincy), Kentucky; Euclid, Ohio; Elkhart and South Bend, Indiana; Lake Michigan and Chicago, Illinois; Madison, Wisconsin; Pipestone, Minnesota; Sioux Falls, Chamberlain, Missouri River, Badlands, Wall, Black Hills, South Dakota; Yellowstone National Park, Wyoming; Rocky Mountains, Montana; Coeur d'Alene and Lewiston, Idaho.

Page 15

1. Sal thinks, "There goes your mother," when she's smoking the pipe.
2. Gram knew that if Gramps treated his dog well, he'd treat her well.
3. Sal's father seems more animated and happy when he's with Mrs. Cadaver.
4. Sal hits the knothole of a tree with a rock.
5. Gram is bitten by a water moccasin.
6. Phoebe and Prudence take their mother for granted, snap at her and demand that she do things for them.
7. Sugar goes on a trip to Idaho to find out who she really is. Students who read ahead may note that she had a stillborn baby and left in order to heal.
8. Sal's father feels that his wife is haunting him in Kentucky.
9. The Town may be "by the banks" of a river.

Page 18

Kentucky—Shawnee, Chickasaw, Cherokee; Ohio—Shawnee; Indiana—Shawnee; Illinois—Illini; Wisconsin—Chippewa; Minnesota—Chippewa; South Dakota—Sioux; Wyoming—Shoshone; Montana— Blackfoot, Crow; Idaho—Coeur d'Alene.

Page 20

1. You can't keep the birds of sadness from flying over your head, but you can keep them from nesting in your hair.
2. Mr. Birkway has the same liveliness, excitement, and passion for stories that Sal observed in her mother.
3. Sal watched her mother eating blackberries, and then kissing a tree. She left behind the imprint of her lips.
4. Sal's father is looking at a photo of himself and his wife, sitting beneath a sugar maple tree.
5. Sal depicts her soul as a maple leaf inside a circle.
6. Sal's house is dirty and confused after her mother leaves.
7. Phoebe's father doesn't think his wife would have made casseroles and frozen them for the family if she'd been kidnapped.
8. Sal's mother's new baby was stillborn.

Page 25

1. Sal feels sorry for Phoebe.
2. Sal notices that dinner with the Finney family reminds her of dinner with her cousins back in Kentucky.
3. Sal understands that sometimes people need to be alone with their sorrow.
4. Gramps teaches Sal to drive on his farm when she is eleven.
5. Sal is terrified by the death in this poem.
6. Phoebe shows Sergeant Bickle the notes from the doorstep, as well as the hair strands.
7. Mrs. Partridge knows their footsteps and the way they smell.
8. The students are angry at each other or amused by what people have revealed about themselves.

Page 27

Crazy Horse was carved by Korczak Ziolkowski, beginning in 1948. His wife continued the project after his death. The project is not yet completed. The monument depicts a Native American hero and his horse. It is located in South Dakota. Students might also visit the Indian Museum and Cultural Center.

Answer Key

Page 27 (*cont.*)

Mount Rushmore was carved by Gutzon Borglum, beginning in 1927. His son continued the project after his death. The memorial was completed in 1941. It depicts the heads of George Washington, Thomas Jefferson, Abraham Lincoln, and Theodore Roosevelt. It is located in South Dakota. Students might also visit Borglum's studio, located near the monument.

Page 28

Aphrodite—goddess of love

Apollo—god of sun/intelligence

Ares—god of war

Artemis—goddess of hunting

Athena—goddess of wisdom

Demeter—goddess of wheat and grain

Dionysius—god of wine

Hades—lord over the world of the dead

Hephaestus—god of fire

Hera—goddess of marriage

Hermes—messenger of the gods

Hestia—goddess of the hearth

Persephone—goddess of maidens

Poseidon—god of the sea

Zeus—ruler of heavens

Page 30

1. Mr. Birkway says that Mrs. Cadaver is his sister and that she lost her husband in an accident.
2. Grams cries because she's happy she got to see Old Faithful.
3. Mr. Birkway apologizes for reading students' journals out loud. Students should answer for themselves how they feel about this.
4. They see Mrs. Winterbottom kissing a young man on the cheek.
5. Ben's mother lives in a psychiatric unit.
6. Mrs. Winterbottom reveals that the young man is her son, whom she put up for adoption.
7. Gram has a stroke.
8. Sal's mother is killed in a bus accident.

Page 32

Coretta Scott King—political activist and wife of Dr. Martin Luther King, Jr.,—four children

Laura Ingalls Wilder—children's writer—one daughter

Florence Griffith Joyner—Olympic runner—one daughter

Marie Curie—scientist— two daughters

Mary Wolstonecraft—feminist writer and teacher— two daughters

Eleanor Roosevelt—political activist and wife of Franklin Delano Roosevelt—six children

Wilma Mankiller—first female in modern history to lead a Native American tribe—two daughters

Abigail Adams—political activist, writer, and wife of John Adams—three sons and two daughters

Margaret Mead—anthropologist—one daughter

Madeleine L'Engle—writer and teacher—three children

Toni Morrison—winner of the Nobel Prize for Literature— two children

Page 43

Matching				True or False
1. h		6. j		1. True
2. g		7. a		2. False
3. d		8. e		3. False
4. b		9. i		4. False
5. c		10. f		5. False

Short Answer

1. Sal's mother leaves both because she gave birth to a stillborn child and needs to heal, and because she wants to know who she is beyond being a wife and mother.
2. Phoebe's mother leaves because she wants to reconnect with the son she gave up for adoption.
3. Sal's father needs to move away from Kentucky, where the memory of his wife haunts him. He moves to Euclid to spend time with Mrs. Cadaver, who was at his wife's side when she died.
4. Sal takes a trip across the country with her grandparents to "follow in her mother's footsteps" and view the place where she died in Lewiston, Idaho.

Essay

Answers will vary. Accept reasonable and well-supported answers.

Page 44

Grade students on their comprehension of the story as evidenced by the lengths of answers and depths of responses.

Page 45

Grade students on comprehension of the story, knowledge of the characters, and creativity.